Copyright 1994 by Science of Spirituality
4 S. 175 Naperville Rd., Naperville, IL 60563
and 2 Canal Road, Vijay Nagar, Delhi 110009 India.

Printed in India

These talks were given by Sant Rajinder Singh Ji Maharaj for the birth centenary celebrations of Sant Kirpal Singh Ji Maharaj (born February 6, 1894) and for the Seventh World Religions Conference held in Delhi, India, February 1-7, 1994. The first message in this book was issued in February 1993 at the inauguration of the centenary year celebration. Sant Rajinder Singh Ji Maharaj is the spiritual head of Science of Spirituality and the President of the World Fellowship of Religions.

Dedicated to
Sant Kirpal Singh Ji Maharaj
and
Sant Darshan Singh Ji Maharaj
whose Light continues to
illuminate humanity's path
towards spiritual unity and peace.

Vision of Spiritual Unity and Peace
by Rajinder Singh

Table of Contents

Message for the Inauguration
 of the Centenary of
 Sant Kirpal Singh Ji Maharaj
 February 6, 1993 — 1

Opening of the Centenary:
 "A Sacred Meeting Place"
 February 1, 1994 — 5

Presidential Address for the Seventh
 World Religions Conference
 February 3, 1994 — 13

International Seminar on
 Peace and the Environment
 February 4, 1994 — 19

International Seminar on
 Spiritual Unity
 February 5, 1994 — 33

Birth Centenary of
 Sant Kirpal Singh Ji Maharaj
 February 6, 1994 — 43

Message for the Inauguration of the Centenary of Sant Kirpal Singh Ji Maharaj (1894-1994)

February 6, 1993

This is a great moment as we inaugurate the centenary year of Sant Kirpal Singh Ji Maharaj, one of the greatest spiritual Masters of all times. This year-long celebration begins in February 1993 and will culminate in the one hundredth anniversary of his birth on February 6, 1994. The centenary of Sant Kirpal Singh Ji Maharaj is a time of reflection and action. It is an opportunity for us to reflect upon his life, his teachings, and his timeless message. It is a time to appreciate the priceless gift of spirituality which he bestowed on the people of the modern world.

This historic year is also a time for action. After reflecting upon his teachings, we need to put his noble ideals into action. He drew up a blueprint to guide us in becoming ideal human beings and transforming this world into a golden paradise of peace, unity, and high values. If we have not yet attained these goals, let us devote ourselves individually and collectively to realize their fulfillment.

Sant Kirpal Singh Ji opened up his treasure house of spirituality to all humanity. He devoted every moment of his life to the pursuit of spiritual truths, deeply exploring the underlying message of each religion and every form of yoga. Through the benign guidance of his own spiritual mentor, Hazur Baba Sawan Singh Ji Maharaj, he distilled the kernel of each religion and yoga so that seekers everywhere could grasp the essential teachings and easily put them into practice in his or her own life. In an age where economic demands require that people spend most of their time earning a living to support themselves and their families, with little available free time to devote to the spiritual search, Sant Kirpal Singh Ji provided a means whereby humanity could tread the spiritual path within the context of modern life. He cut through the rites, rituals, and arduous practices that would take one years to master, and presented a quick, natural, and easy method to realize one's self and realize God in one's lifetime. Sant Kirpal Singh Ji presented the timeless teachings of Surat Shabd Yoga or Sant Mat in a scientific way so that people who were born in the technological age could understand them. Through tours, books, satsang gatherings, and conferences, he made these teachings available throughout the world. He taught a method of meditation on the inner Light and Sound which would help the soul rise above the physical world, enter into high spiritual realms, and travel on the divine current of Light and Sound back to God. Union of the soul with God is the ultimate goal of life, and its attainment floods one with eternal bliss and happiness. Seekers received from Sant Kirpal Singh Ji a firsthand spiritual experience of the inner Light and Sound which provided them with the inner proof to start their journey homeward. He lovingly guided aspirants through every step of the spiritual journey, steering them clear of pitfalls and obstacles along the way.

One of the hallmarks of Sant Kirpal Singh Ji's message was the need to become ideal human beings. Along with practicing meditation, he taught people how to develop the qualities that reflect their divinity as children of the Lord. He wanted them to recognize that each one is a child of God and should reflect the divine virtues in his or her daily life. He himself exemplified those virtues in his own life and showed humanity that "what one can do, another could also do." His entire life was one long saga of selfless service, compassion, and love for his fellow beings. Even though he had a career and a family to look after, he always made it top priority to spend time in meditation and in serving those in need. He visited the sick in hospitals and in their homes. He attended to numerous people who came to him for help and guidance. He loved and served all who came to him irrespective of their religion, nationality, or social status. To him, all were children of the one Creator.

This lofty angle of vision moved him to bring together heads of various religions who previously would not even sit together for a discussion. Through the four World Religions Conferences over which he presided, he tried to show the underlying unity of all religions and to bring about peace where there was previously bigotry and prejudice. Sant Kirpal Singh Ji convened the first Unity of Man Conference--now called the Human Unity Conference--in which people of not only all religions, but those who were theists as well as atheists, could sit together in love and worship the one Father.

Let us reflect upon his spiritual message, his call for unity and peace, and his exhortation to mold ourselves into ideal children of the Lord. Our Gracious Master, Sant Darshan Singh Ji Maharaj, had wished this centenary to be one of the great events of all times. Let us make it a memorable event for our souls as well, and spend this upcoming centenary year putting Sant Kirpal Singh Ji Maharaj's goals and visions of love, unity, and peace into action.

Opening of the Centenary: "A Sacred Meeting Place"

February 1, 1994

It is befitting that we begin the birth centenary of our Beloved Master, Sant Kirpal Singh Ji Maharaj, here at Sawan Ashram--this meeting place on which he planted the seeds of spirituality. He began his mission here with the sacred trust given to him by Hazur Baba Sawan Singh Ji Maharaj to plant the seeds of spirituality in every heart. It was on this land that he built a meeting place where members of each religion could sit together in love, where heads of all religions could meet to bring about peace, where souls could learn the method to meet God within themselves, and where all humanity could meet as brothers and sisters in the Lord.

Many of us would have remembered the divine moments when we sat upon these grounds and gazed into the love-filled eyes of our beloved Master, Sant Kirpal Singh Ji Maharaj. Many of us would have recalled the melodious voice of love that flowed out from his lips. Many of us would have recalled the eternal moments of intoxication we experienced being in his uplifting spiritual radiation. Many of us would have recalled the miraculous transformation we experienced in our lives by sitting in his holy presence. For those who met Sant Kirpal Singh Ji, returning here is a homecoming to a meeting place filled with his remembrance.

For those who did not meet him, this place is one at which we can lay our gratitude, for it was he who not only planted the seeds of spirituality but spread them far and wide to reach people from all parts of the world. If we are sitting here today, it is because of the groundwork lovingly laid by the Beloved Master making spirituality accessible to each of us.

We see before us people from every inhabited continent. We bear the flags of different nations, but our hearts are united as citizens of one nation, the nation of love, which Sant Kirpal Singh Ji founded. This was the sacred land upon which he taught us the universal language of love. He gave out that message in many different ways so that it could be received by people from all walks of life. He broadcast it to followers of each religion, to religious heads, and to all souls, whether theists or atheists. That message was that God is love, each of us as soul is also love, and the way back to God is through love. He invited people from all over the world to come to this meeting place and discover the love within themselves.

This was a sacred meeting place for religious heads. Through Sant Kirpal Singh Ji Maharaj's work as founder of Ruhani Satsang and as president of the World Fellowship of Religions, he presided over four World Religions Conferences in which he invited heads of all religions to sit together. This was a landmark achievement, for it was accomplished during a time when religious heads would neither talk to each other, nor sit on the same platform. But his example of love and respect for all religions touched the hearts of religious leaders and they came here to sit together in love and to find the underlying unity of their respective religions. He laid the foundation for interreligious dialogue. If today we see people of all religions meeting with each other, it was due to the groundwork he laid on this sacred land.

This was also a sacred meeting place between members of all religions. People of all religions came here with the common goal of realizing their selves and realizing God. He taught spirituality as a science, one that could be practiced by people of all faiths and religions. Thus, we found here, people of all religions sitting side by side in meditation. We found people of all religions and nationalities filled with so much intoxication and love they would embrace each other as brothers and sisters. In his langar, people of all colors and religious faiths would sit side by side partaking of their meals. We would see people forming friendships and bonds of love with people of all nationalities and religions. During decades when prejudice and bigotry were rampant, he created a haven in which all barriers between human beings were torn asunder, and people related to each other as children of one God.

This was a sacred meeting place where souls could meet God. He himself had discovered at the feet of his own Master, Hazur Baba Sawan Singh Ji Maharaj, the method by which the soul could gain communion with the Lord. He himself searched high and low for a way back to God. Before he found his Master, he had delved in many a yoga, read every book he could find on mysticism, and met many a teacher. He prayed with deep intensity and yearning to be shown the way to meet the Lord. He did not want to waste his life in methods that would not grant him the beatific vision of God. The Lord finally answered his prayers and led him to the holy feet of the great Hazur. Hazur initiated him into the path of meditation on the inner Light and Sound, Surat Shabd Yoga. Through this method of meditation, Sant Kirpal Singh Ji's search for God culminated in his attaining God-realization. Sant Kirpal Singh Ji was commissioned by Hazur before he left the body to grant initiation to seekers after truth. From that point on, he worked tirelessly to make this gift available to all seekers after truth. He shared this gift freely, considering it a sacred gift from God, like air, water, and sunlight. He started Sawan Ashram as a place where people could learn the meditation technique. His love for humanity was so great that it was not enough for him to sit here and wait for people to come to him. He went out and sought every soul who was crying for God. At first he went visiting the houses of interested seekers in Delhi, sitting with them for long hours in their homes, enlightening them with spirituality. Then he went to villages and towns throughout the length and breadth of India. He wanted to bestow the spiritual gifts with both hands, and so he went even further than India. In

1955 he was the first Master of Sant Mat to journey across the ocean to the West, spreading the seeds of spirituality to Europe and the Americas. He made three world tours to share the blessings he had received from his Master. Wishing to reach yet more people, he began writing books and seeing that they were translated so that the teachings of Hazur Baba Sawan Singh Ji could reach even the remotest corners of the globe.

    This was also a sacred meeting place where all members of humanity could meet together in love. In 1974 he brought the work of peace and unity to even a higher level. He convened the first Unity of Man Conference. He felt that previous conferences only joined people at the level of religion. He wanted to join all members of humanity, whether they were theists or atheists. At his historic conference, convened on this sacred land, we found humanity sitting together, irrespective of whether they were believers in God or not. For Sant Kirpal Singh Ji, all were brothers and sisters irrespective of whether they followed one religion or another, or whether they followed any religion at all. He exemplified the highest form of love on earth--the love that recognized each being as a soul, as a child of God, and as brothers and sisters.

    Let us look around ourselves now. Look to your right, look to your left, turn and look behind and in front of you. Look at the diversity among the people at this assembly. There are people from many nations, people from all religions, people from all spiritual beliefs, and people who are agnostics and atheists. There are people of all ages, people of all social backgrounds, people of all walks of life. If we are sitting here together in peace and unity, it is because of the work he began on this sacred land. Our sitting here today is a testament to the mission for which he lived--the mission of love, unity, and peace. Let us offer our gratitude towards him for opening the floodgates of spirituality and peace. Let us thank him with all our heart and soul for the gifts he gave to humanity and the gifts he gave to each of us.

Let us also offer our gratitude to the Gracious Master, Sant Darshan Singh Ji Maharaj. In the last few years of his life, he spoke often about this centenary year that we are celebrating today. He knew he would not be among us but he laid the plan for this centenary. He told us that this would be the greatest event of our century. His love for Sant Kirpal Singh Ji Maharaj was so great that he wanted his name to be on the lips of every soul in creation. Let us fulfill his wish and carry the name of Kirpal to every nook and corner of the earth. Let us not only carry the words on our lips, but carry his teachings in our every action. Let every person who meets us ask us from whom did we learn to be the abode of love, peace, and unity. Let us reply that we learned the lesson of love, peace and unity from Sant Kirpal Singh Ji Maharaj.

Let us go forth from this sacred land carrying high the banner of Sant Kirpal Singh Ji's message of love. Let it be seen from the peaks of the Himalayan mountains, from the Alps of Europe, from the Rockies of North America and the Andes of South America. Let it be seen from the four oceans of the world. Let it be seen from the tropical rainforests of Africa, Asia, and South America. Let it be seen by every soul in creation. And let it not only be seen, but let it be lived every moment of our lives. In this way we can truly celebrate this centenary year of one of the greatest Masters who ever walked this earth.

Let us reach out and touch the soil of this sacred place and remember the one whose holy feet once walked here. And let that remembrance carry us into his arms waiting for us within. He has not left us. He is still here with us this very day, smiling at each of us, radiating his love to each of us, and holding out his arms to each of us to embrace us and carry us to the sacred land of God within. May we never forget our beloved Kirpal, for he has never forgotten any of us.

I would like to end with this beautiful verse by Sant Darshan Singh Ji Maharaj written in 1955 in honor of Sant Kirpal Singh Ji Maharaj's birthday celebration:

> Blessed was the day when the Eternal Light manifested itself in this transitory world in the form of the Glorious Resplendent Master.
>
> Blessed was the day when all the beauty and grace of the heavens condensed themselves in the form of the Beloved of the Universe.
>
> Blessed was the day when the ambrosia-laden clouds of Divine Grace poured forth showers on this parched earth.

Blessed was the day when on the arrival of the Universal Cupbearer, the goblet was in ecstasy and the cup fell in trance.

With the advent of Kirpal, the tavern of God overflowed with vintage divine.

He is the Universal Cupbearer, He is the Nectar of Immortality, He is the Light of God.

Presidential Address of the Seventh World Religions Conference

February 3, 1994

Meditation and Prayer for Inner and Outer Peace

I would like to welcome all of you who have come to this great conference. This Seventh World Religions Conference is an historic event for it falls on the Birth Centenary of Sant Kirpal Singh Ji Maharaj, the founder-president of the first World Religions Conference. Sant Kirpal Singh Ji Maharaj and Acharya Muni Sushil Kumar Ji, the founder of the World Fellowship of Religions, had the vision and foresight to set the stage for this common platform upon which people of all religions can sit together in the spirit of peace, fellowship and love, as brothers and sisters in the divine Power that created us all.

The Seventh World Fellowship of Religions Conference was convened to unite all religions and faiths through universal meditation and prayer for attaining inner and outer peace. At the heart of each religion is the emphasis on prayer and meditation as a way to achieve peace both within and without. The Conference aims at finding the unifying factors at the core of each religion as a bridge between all humanity. The focus at this Conference will be the exploration of the various methods of prayer and meditation found in all faiths and how each religion reveres these methods as a way to achieve peace.

By attaining inner and outer peace, the world can see an end to war, conflicts, devastation, inhumanity, poverty, and destruction of the environment. By finding a way to bring peace to individuals as well as the entire planet, we will usher in an age of non-violence, kindness, tolerance, respect, understanding, and a sharing of resources to see that every man, woman, and child has food to eat, proper health care, and the freedom to live their lives free of the threat of criminal acts or of war.

In the past twenty years, peace movements, spiritual movements, and ecological movements have been advocating the need for world peace and human unity. Through their efforts millions of people have turned to a life of prayer, meditation, and the attainment of inner and outer peace. But we still find millions of people on our planet engaged in global conflicts over their religious beliefs. There are still countless deaths and even massacres of whole peoples because they worship God by different names and through different customs. All the efforts of peace groups can only help our planet to a limited degree. The responsibility of peace lies in the hands of our religious leaders who have the power to turn back the arrows of hatred, who have the power to lay down arms against other religious groups, who have the power to offer instead flowers of peace to all people, irrespective of their religious beliefs. If the heads of all major religions: Christianity, Judaism, Hinduism, Buddhism, Islam, Sikhism, Taoism, Shintoism, Sufism, Zoroastrianism, and other faiths declare a moratorium on religious intolerance and religious war and instead exhort their followers to pray and meditate together for inner and outer peace, world unity and harmony will prevail on our planet.

This Conference will provide opportunities for religious leaders and followers to share the importance of meditation and prayer in their own faiths and to engage in dialogue on how meditation can be used as a unifying force to bring together all people on our planet in love, tolerance, and peace. The fruits of this conference will be a garden of peace on earth.

The by-products of these deliberations will be an end to violence, inhumanity, war and conflict. People will join together to find peaceful solutions to world problems such as poverty, hunger, inadequate health care, illiteracy, and social ills. Humanity will become more aware of the need for ecology, conservation, and protection of the environment and natural resources, and the preservation of all forms of life. Our world will be filled with religious tolerance and mutual cooperation among all people. We will see an improved quality of life on our planet brought about by the combined, synergistic efforts and exchange of ideas among people of all nations and religions.

Along this historic peace march today, reminiscent of the march that took place at the Unity of Man Conference convened in 1974 by Sant Kirpal Singh Ji Maharaj, we passed places of worship of different religions. Was it not beautiful to see how many different ways people worship the One Lord. Is not a garden more beautiful when it is decorated with flowers of different colors and fragrances? Similarly, we are all flowers in the garden of the Lord. We have different colored hair, eyes, and skin; we speak different languages, follow the culture of different countries, and worship according to the customs of our different religions, yet we all worship the one Creator.

As Sant Darshan Singh Ji Maharaj said in one of his verses:

> We are but drops of the same fountain of divine beauty;
>
> We are but waves on the great river of love.
>
> We are diverse blossoms in the Garden of the Lord, Who have gathered in the same valley of Light.
>
> We who dwell on this earth belong to one humanity;
>
> There is but one God, and we are all His children.

Let us march forth to overcome the storms of strife;

Let us march forth to light the lamp of Universal Love.

Let the lotus of renewed aspirations blossom in our hearts,

And let those long-divided embrace one another.

If all those who have been divided by the outer labels of our religions can embrace each other in love, we will usher in a golden age of peace and spirituality for the upcoming millennium. We have gathered together at this sacred moment of time. Future generations will look back upon this event and the groundwork that we are laying for the next millennium. When our progeny remembers us, do we not wish them to say that it was we, the leaders of this time, who put an end to all wars and set humanity on the golden road to peace? The religious leaders hold the key to world peace. It is they who have the power to stop the tides of war and to allow peace to prevail on the planet. It is the hopes of the Seventh World Religions Conference to complete the work of all previous conferences by using the key given to humanity by the Creator--meditation and prayer--as the only solution to inner and outer peace on the planet. Meditation is the unifying force that can knit us all together. The power of God flows within each of us. God's light shines in each one of us. The music of

God sings in each one of us.

On this day, the opening of this Seventh World Religions Conference and the Birth Centenary of Sant Kirpal Singh Ji Maharaj, let each of us hold high the godly lamp within us. Let each of us sing the song of peace and unity in our hearts. Let this godly light and music guide our every thought, word, and action. Let our combined prayers and meditations resound through all creation as one song to God: "Let there be unity, let there be love, let there be peace."

May God hear our combined prayers and bless us with eternal peace and love.

International Seminar on Peace and the Environment

February 4, 1994

We have witnessed more scientific and technological advances in the past four decades than in all previous recorded history. Scientists have uncovered many of the laws which govern nature itself. The more they learn about the mysteries of nature, the more they marvel at the perfection of the universe. Many now proclaim that the universe cannot be haphazard, but must be the design of some Higher Power.

There is a perfect balance in nature. Our world, our environment, and nature itself form a living interdependent system. Seen from the proper perspective, there is no division or duality. Life itself appears to be a single unit. It is a living, conscious entity. It was formed by the hands of the Creator and was animated by His life breath.

The perfect balance of nature which has maintained life on our planet for millions of years is being threatened by the very technology that has transformed the modern world. Every day the media reports new threats to the environment. The air we breathe, the water we drink, and the land from which we derive our food are all progressively polluted. The very atmosphere protecting the earth is endangered. The concern for the ecology of our planet is not limited to any one country or part of the world. We face a global problem.

Concern for the ecology has become one of the main preoccupations of the world. If we look into the etymology of the word "ecology" we find that it comes from the Greek language. The Greek work "oikos" means "house" or "dwelling place." The word "ology" means "the study of." So the word originally meant "the study of our house or dwelling place." Today when we think of the study of our dwelling place, our thoughts turn to the earth and Mother Nature. We may divide this study into four areas: understanding the cycles of nature, becoming aware of the effects of pollution, learning how to restore nature to its pristine beauty, and putting into practice methods to preserve the purity of nature. We may think of these four areas as: natural cycles, pollution, restoration, and preservation.

There is another way of understanding the word ecology. Saints and mystics refer to our home or dwelling place as the physical body which God Himself has made. The indweller of this house is the soul. The scriptures tell us that we have a responsibility to maintain and preserve the purity and beauty of the soul and its dwelling place. Unfortunately, we have largely ignored our spiritual side, and have sacrificed its purity for the sake of the transitory world.

I would like to examine the ecology of the

soul. The same four areas of study apply to the inner and the outer ecology. There are fundamental laws and cycles that apply to the spirit just as to nature. We can gain an awareness of how pollution affects us within as well as how it affects the world around us. We can learn how to restore nature and our own self to their original beauty. And we can put into practice methods to preserve our spiritual purity.

Cycles

All life forms one perfect tapestry. Fundamental laws and cycles underlie existence. The life cycle in nature is an example of perfect interconnectedness. Water from the seas evaporates and turns into water vapor. In this process, impurities and minerals are left behind. The vapor forms into clouds, which are blown across the land. As the clouds meet cool air, the water condenses into water droplets, and these pour down as rain or snow which nourishes life. For countless ages this cycle has brought water from the abundant oceans to the land so that animals and people can have fresh water to drink and green plants can flourish.

With all our advances, we have not devised a technology that can duplicate the method by which green plants convert sunlight, carbon dioxide, and water into food and oxygen. Through this simple process the earth receives a fresh supply of oxygen, necessary for all life, and an inexhaustible store of food is available.

There is a perfect design in Nature. Even death helps to bring forth life. When plants and animals die, their decomposed bodies provide essential minerals for crops. After millions of years the decomposed material forms into energy-producing fossil fuels.

The ecological system which God created on our earth is so unique that ours is the only habitable planet in our solar system.

Like other natural cycles--such as the water cycle, the plant cycle, and the fossil fuel cycle--there is also a cycle of the soul. The soul's journey began with the creation of the Universe, and it has been in motion ever since.

The scriptures tell us that in the beginning God was all alone. He was an Ocean of all blissful consciousness. Then He decided to become many from one. This thought set in motion a vibration, which resulted in two principles: Light and Sound. All scriptures speak of this Light and Sound by various names. This Word or Naam was the God-into-expression Power. It created various planes of existence, from the purely spiritual plane of Sach Khand, the spiritual-material regions of the supra-causal plane, the causal plane, and the astral plane, to the material realms of this physical plane. It created human beings and all other species of life. It is this creative Power which keeps the universe running in perfect symmetry and harmony, holding planets in their orbit and the stars in the heavens.

The soul is a spark of that creative principle. It is the enlivening force within us. As long as the soul inhabits the body, the body is alive. When the soul departs a body, the person dies. When God created the universes, He separated souls from Himself to inhabit the worlds. Thus, began the cycle of the soul. For aeons it has been inhabiting the various planes of creation, taking up residence in one life form or another. When one existence is over, it returns to another. As a plant dies in the winter to regenerate in the spring, so does the soul transmigrate. When one life is over, it begins another, in a new form. Nothing is lost in nature. The soul, being a spark of the immortal God, never dies. It simply moves from one life to another.

God, while separating souls from Himself, has also provided a way for souls to return to Him. This way back to Him is through the current of Naam or Word. But, in the scheme of creation, it has been so ordained that the soul does not remember its past existence until it has achieved spiritual evolution. A cloud of forgetfulness covers each soul when it enters a new birth. It has also forgotten its true nature as soul, a drop of God. It has identified itself with the mind and body. Instead of seeking the way back to its Source, it is attracted to the temptations of the world.

The knowledge of our true self lies buried in the deepest recesses of our innermost soul. Like a diamond buried deep within the earth, or the layers of rich oil lying far below the earth's surface, our most precious riches, the soul, lies buried beneath layers of mind, matter, and illusion. We need to tap it during our present life span to uncover our greatest resource.

Pollution

The next aspect of inner and outer ecology is pollution. Like air and water, the soul has an innate beauty of its own. It is made of the same essence as God. It has been said, "God is love, the soul, being of the same essence as God, is love, and the way back to God is also through love."

For millions of years our earth has had clean air and fresh flowing waters. But our exploitation of the planet has sullied these natural resources. We have polluted our air, water, and soil and are destroying the earth's ozone layer, its forests, and its animals. In a similar fashion, our insatiable appetite for gratifying our senses has polluted the natural purity of the soul.

Many of us think that our seat of intelligence is the brain. But the brain is merely a tool, like a complex computer, through which the soul communicates with and receives impressions from the outer world. The operator behind the machinery of the body and mind is the soul. The soul should have been in control of the mind and body, but the situation has been reversed. The soul is now led by the mind and has been caught up in the sensory impressions of the world.

The sights and sounds, the aromas and tastes, and the intriguing sensations of the world have attracted our attention, which is the outer expression of our soul. As a result our attention has been dragged outward through the nine doors of the body: the two eyes, two ears, two nostrils, the mouth, and two organs below. The mind, being a lover of enjoyment, has pulled our consciousness into the physical world, and we have forgotten our true self.

We pass our life caught up in sensuous and worldy pleasures. We have come to believe that the purpose of our life is to amass worldly and material gifts such as wealth, possessions, relations, name and fame, and power. We forget that none of these can go with us when we die. They are as vaporous as mirages in the desert. We depart from the world as we came in--as soul, devoid of any material belongings.

For many, this realization occurs too late. The worldly desires and sensuous pleasures settle like dust on the pure soul. After aeons of coming and going in the world, our soul has become so covered with the pollution of worldly impressions that we cannot recognize it. But there are some fortunate souls who experience an awakening. They come to realize that there is a spiritual significance to life. An innate desire for immortality moves these souls to solve the mystery of life and death. When the questions of who we are, why are we here, and where do we go arise within us, a spiritual spark is ignited. We cannot rest until we find the answer. A sincere cry issues forth from deep within us, and we pray to the Lord for help and guidance.

Restoring the Beauty of the Soul

The third aspect of this subject is restoring the beauty of the soul. The ecologists who work to clean our polluted air and water and free those animals trapped in the muck or oil spills, are the environmental heroes and heroines of our times. We also have in our world ecologists of the soul. These beings have realized the pristine beauty of the spirit and are aware of those pollutants which cover it with layers of dirt and filth. They too are working constantly to find those seekers trapped in worldly desires so they can be set free.

The divine ecologists are better known to us as the saints and mystics, prophets and spiritual teachers who have come throughout the ages. They themselves have become pure and free of all that pollutes the soul. And they are able to free others as well. They have liberated their soul from the limits of the physical body and have soared above on the pure, divine stream back to God.

Saints and mystics can hear the cries of the souls yearning to be free. A spiritual teacher can show us our true nature. He teaches us how to analyze ourself so that we can separate our soul or self from the layers of mind, matter, and illusion that cover it. He does this through spiritual initiation and by teaching us a method of meditation.

Preserving the Natural Beauty of the Soul

The fourth aspect of inner and outer ecology is preserving the natural beauty of the soul. Once we have a direct experience of the inner Light and Sound, we realize that we are not the body but are soul. We realize that there is a higher Reality within us. It is the beginning of our journey to our true Home.

Spiritual Adepts teach us those practices which will help us clean off the grime of ages. There are two things which will help to purify us faster: the cleansing Water of Naam and ethical living.

Once we are taught the method of meditation and are given a contact with the Light and Sound of God, we need to engage in the inner practices every day. We need to daily set aside some time from our work-a-day life to commune with the current of Light and Sound within. The more we listen to the inner sound, the more our soul is cleansed, and the worldly impressions are washed away.

The second helping factor they teach us is to lead an ethical life. In order to progress on our spiritual journey within, we need to overcome anger, lust, greed, attachment, and ego. These are the five pollutants that cover the purity of the soul. They drag our attention into the world. If we analyze these five negative traits, we find they are all motivated by our desire for transitory and worldly pleasures. For example, we become angry when anything interferes with attaining our worldly desires. Lust is caused by the desire to gratify our senses. Greed results from our insatiable desire to amass either possessions, riches, power, or name and fame. When we attain any of these we become attached to them, and forget the spiritual values and our spiritual nature. Ego arises from pride of our transitory attainments: pride of wealth, worldly knowledge, and power.

To help us overcome these five negative qualities, we need to review our thoughts, words, and deeds each day. This gives us a realistic picture of the pollutants which defile the soul. We can then resolve to improve the following day.

Saints lay great emphasis on ethical living and speak of it as a stepping-stone to spirituality. Sant Kirpal Singh Ji used to say that it is difficult to become a human being in the true sense; but once we have accomplished this, it is relatively easy to find God. What is required is nothing short of the total transformation in one's life.

To me, ecology means that if we are polluting our world it means that we do not care about anyone else. If we care about our family, if we care about our neighbor, we would not do anything to pollute the environment and make life difficult for other human beings. The whole problem of ecology could be solved if we as humans start to realize that each form of creation inhabiting the earth is an embodied soul. If we realize that the soul in us is the same soul that inhabits every being, whether plant or animal, and comes from the same Source, from the same Oversoul, from God, then we would care about and love every being. We would see the Light of God in each living thing. And what does love mean? Love means actually caring about someone else. Love does not mean just a physical attraction. The real divine love, really having love for someone, means you care about them. And caring about someone means that you do not want to make their life difficult. If all of us in this world start thinking of everyone else as our brothers and sisters, as being of the same essence as God that we are, then we would not do anything to harm other people. We would try to live our lives so that we do not pollute the environment in which other people have to live. Through the process of connecting ourselves to the Light and Sound of God, we begin to realize the Light of God in all beings and we start believing in the brotherhood of humanity and the Fatherhood of God. Once we attain that state, it reflects in our own lives and helps the society and the country in which we live and the whole world.

If our planet, with its interdependent ecological systems, is to survive, we have to learn to live in harmony with all creation. We have to develop a kind of respect for our environment in which we do not ignore the claims and contributions of even the tiniest of creatures. Ecologists are sensitive enough to avoid altering anything in the environment which will upset the balance of nature. Similarly, when we advance spiritually, we begin to move through life with sensitivity. We no longer injure the feelings of others. We treat those we come in contact with, with love and gentleness. As we develop the positive virtues and continue meditating on the Holy Naam, we find that the imperfections and pollutants that covered us will fall away and we are restored to our original purity.

Dedicated ecologists feel a great sense of duty to work towards preserving the purity of the environment. They want to do what they can to live in harmony with nature. Similarly, those who discover themselves and realize God also feel a sense of responsibility. The attainment of the spiritual riches is not an end in itself. One develops a deep love for all creation. One sees the hand of God behind every blade of grass. This respect and love for life manifests itself in selfless service.

Those who realize God do not leave the world to spend it in isolated meditation. They develop an innate desire to serve their fellow beings, and all life. This may come as a surprise to many in the West who think that spirituality is life-negating and meant for recluses and monks. Sant Darshan Singh Ji used to term that approach as "negative mysticism." Sant Darshan Singh Ji coined the term "positive mysticism." This approach means that while pursuing our spiritual goals, we continue to perform our obligations to our family, community, nation, and the world, and we do so to the best of our ability. We continue to earn our livelihood honestly so we can maintain ourselves and our family, and can help those in need. We remain in the religion into which we are born, but live up to its true purpose--knowing ourselves and realizing God. We raise our families, and see that they receive the best educational opportunities in life. We try to attain the best of both worlds. We strive to excel in all our endeavors. While living and working in the world, though, we are always mindful of our spiritual goal.

Let us devote our time to the spiritual practices, to prayer and meditation, so we can recover our innate God-given beauty. Once we develop it, we will reflect that radiance to all those with whom we come in contact. We will in fact shower that love on all living things and on our planet earth.

By restoring the ecological health of our soul, we will be purifying and uplifting all creation. Then, this world will return to the divine stage of godly bliss and ecstasy for which we were created.

During this conference we have the opportunity to make a commitment to care for our planet, our fellow human beings, and all life forms. We have a chance to put our heads together to find peaceful solutions to the problems facing our planet. These environmental issues facing us can be solved if people of all nationalities and religions work together and use their combined talents, energies, and resources to make the world a better place. We all share the same earth, the same sky, and the same resources. We have learned that all of us are interdependent. If one nation has ecological problems, it affects all other countries on earth. This is our opportunity for leaders of all religions and nationalities to set the example for the entire world by working together to find solutions to global crises. It is up to us to save the earth not only for our children and grandchildren but for posterity.

During his lifetime, Sant Kirpal Singh Ji Maharaj worked for what he called man-service, land-service, and animal-service. When he built Manav Kendra, part of his ideal was land-service. He taught the importance of developing the land for agriculture and farmland to meet the needs of the people. He had a keen interest in preserving trees. When constructing buildings, Sant Kirpal Singh Ji would build them in such a way as to avoid cutting down trees. Thus, we find in his buildings trees left standing, even though they grew through the middle of rooms.

Along with land-service, he encouraged animal-service. From childhood Sant Kirpal Singh Ji had an innate sense of the importance of non-violence to animals. In fact, he became a vegetarian as a young boy, refusing meat that his non-vegetarian parents offered him. He taught his followers to also become vegetarians. Thus, they do not eat any meat, fish, fowl, or eggs, both fertile and infertile. He taught that God has provided humanity with enough food in the form of plants and there is no need to take the life of our younger brothers and sisters in God. He had respect for all forms of life. When building Manav Kendra, construction workers complained of the large amount of snakes that were unearthed. They wanted to destroy the snakes, but Sant Kirpal Singh Ji stopped them. He said that it was due to the digging that they were uprooted from their homes. He then advised that the snakes be gently picked up with sticks and taken to other fields to live out their lives. Thus, during the construction not a single snake was killed. His example has inspired thousands of people around the world to lead their lives with the same regard for the planet and for all forms of life.

If we can realize the divinity that enlivens all life forms on our planet, we will spread peace and love wherever we go. Let me conclude with some verses from the poem, "The Cry of the Soul," written by the great Master, Sant Darshan Singh Ji Maharaj:

> We are but drops of the same fountain of divine beauty,
>
> We are but waves on the great river of love.
>
> We are diverse blossoms in the Garden of the Lord,
>
> We have gathered in the same Valley of Light.
>
> We who dwell on this earth belong to one humanity,
>
> There is but one God, and we are all His children.

International Seminar on Spiritual Unity

February 5, 1994

Every day throughout the world there are meetings and conferences for a multitude of purposes. There are conferences on science, education, health, welfare, technology, business, and numerous other topics. Of all the conferences for which people get together, the one for which we are gathering today, spiritual unity, is the most significant one in which humanity can be involved. Why? Spiritual unity is the mission statement for which every human being was brought into this world. Spiritual unity is the purpose for which God created the human form and enlivened each with the soul. Spiritual unity is the lesson for which souls were sent down into this world. Spiritual unity is the goal that God seeks for each one of us.

Our Original Nature is Unity

Each religion recognizes a divine Power or Force which brought about creation. Some may call it God, Allah, Bhagwan, Wahiguru, the Lord, and many other names. Some refer to it as a Creative Power. By whatever name we call that Power, all religions recognize it as our Source. All religions also recognize the existence of the soul that enlivens us and that the soul is of the same essence as God. Many scriptures speak of God as an ocean of love, consciousness, and bliss. It is said that in the beginning God was one, and then wished to be many. With that thought, parts of that one were separated and sent to this world as souls. If we each trace our spiritual roots, we will find that at one time we each were connected at the level of the soul in the vast, unlimited, unbounded ocean of the Creator.

Divisions Among People Caused by Forgetting Our True Nature

When we came into this world, we identified ourselves with our body and mind. We came to think of ourselves as the name which our parents gave us, as the religion to which our parents belonged, and to the country into which our physical body lived. The more we identified with these outer labels, the more forgetful we became of our true essence as soul, a part of God. God made humanity, and humanity made divisions. We became identified with the outer customs of our country and religion. We learned a particular language, followed certain customs regarding dress and the way we address each other, and participated in certain rites and rituals of our outer religions. Climatic differences may have influenced the way we worship. In some places, in which water is in abundance, people may wash their hands before prayer. In other places, in which water is scarce, people may wash their hands with sand before prayer. Due to differences in language, people refer to God by different names and offer prayers in different languages.

It is the nature of human beings to take pride in their own way of doing things. Thus each nation and each religion thinks of its own culture and customs as the best and begins to denigrate those from other cultures and religions. Instead of differences being a source of beauty, diversity, and joy, they became a bed of bigotry, intolerance, and hatred. Thus, throughout history we find time and again religious wars bringing untold death, destruction, and misery. We find throughout history people of all religions at one time or another killing in the name of God. We find even followers of the same religious founder divided into different sects within the same religion engaged in religious persecution and wars with each other!

Is it not a tragedy that people kill in the name of the Lord, even though every saint and religious founder who came taught their followers non-violence and love for all? If we make a deep study of each religion and study the sayings of the saints and prophets, we will find that they each taught one lesson: the lesson of love, peace, and unity. Can anyone find any saint who taught otherwise? If we study the lives of the great founders of all religions, we find that they did not come for one particular religious group--they opened their doors to all humanity. Each of the great saints recognized the unity underlying all humanity. Each of them had regard for the teachings of the previous saints. Who is responsible for the sorry state of affairs we have found in our history books? Surely it was not the religious founders, saints, and prophets. If we truly understood their teachings as found in the scriptures that they wrote or passed down to us, we would find the blueprint by which we can live our lives and bring peace and unity to this planet.

How to Find our Essential Unity

Each of the saints and prophets gave to humanity directions and guidelines by which we could recognize our spiritual unity. They exhorted us to go within to find our soul and to realize God. If we study each religion, we will find a method taught to humanity by which we could go within. Some call this process of inversion as prayer, contemplation, or meditation. Each religion lays out an esoteric practice by which followers can realize their self and God. Unfortunately, over time, the esoteric teachings have been lost or forgotten. Most people tend to practice the exoteric or outer side of religions. They may go on pilgrimages, perform certain sacred practices, and read scriptures. But how many people actually sit in silent prayer, meditation, and contemplation leading to a divine, first-hand experience of their soul and God? It was to help people find the soul and God that religions first came into being. No founder came to earth to start a religion. They came to teach a method by which souls could reunite with God. It was only after they left that the followers made a religion in their name. But if we trace the purpose for which they lived and taught, we will find it was simply to put each soul in touch with God.

If we wish to be true followers of our religion, we will trace the esoteric core, the teachings given out by the saints and prophets, and begin to put them into practice. That teaching was to regain our spiritual unity. In each religion we find that the method taught to return to God was to connect with the God Power within us. Each religion calls this Power of God by different names. In the Hindu scriptures it is called Naad, Jyoti or Shruti. The Buddhists call it Sonorous Light. The Muslims call it Kalma. The Sufis call it Sauti-i-Sarmadi or Baang-i-Aasmani. The Zoroastrians call it Sarosha. In the Bible it is called the Holy Word. The ancient Greeks called it Logos. The Sikhs call it Naam or Shabd. In Theosophy it is called the Voice of Silence. In English it is translated as the Light and Sound of God. Each religion spoke of the necessity of the soul connecting with this power of God to travel on it like a stream back to its Source, the Creator.

By a process of meditation or concentration we can contact that Light and Sound within us. It is reverberating within us all the time. We can see it and hear it when our attention is focussed at a point known as the third or single eye, the tisra til, the shiv netra, the divya chakshu, or the tenth door or chakra. Christ said, "If thine eye be single, thy whole body shall be full of light." It is at this single eye that we can connect with the godly Light and travel on it back to our Creator.

Scriptures of the past are filled with accounts of those who came in contact with the godly Light through prayer and meditation. They speak of the transformation they underwent. They describe the Light as being all love, peace, and bliss. Once they were touched by the Light, they were filled with a love that changed their life. They saw God's love everywhere. They saw God's love in everyone. And they recognized that we were all knit together as one human family in the same Father. Even today, we read of accounts of people who had near-death experiences, whose body underwent clinical death, yet their soul rose above the body and entered the Light. Each of them spoke of the Light as an all-embracing Love, a love so warm and fulfilling that they never experienced anything like it on earth. They each spoke of how that love and Light transformed their lives and inculcated in them a love for all humanity.

Once we contact the Light within, we too can partake of that divine love. We will then see that Light of God shining in all beings, in all people, in all animals, in all creation. We will then recognize our essential unity and we will have love for all.

How Finding our Spiritual Unity Can Lead to Peace

When we can see God's Light in every person, every animal, every flower, in every atom of creation, we recognize our spiritual unity. It is not something we merely speak about. It is a love that we experience and feel. It is the same love we may feel for our own parents, children, or spouses. We begin to love all as members of our own family. When we take every being in creation as our brothers and sisters, we treat them with the same love, kindness, and respect with which we treat our own family. That is why Sant Darshan Singh Ji Maharaj wrote in a verse:

> Embrace every man as your own
> And shower your love freely wherever you go.

We shower love to all we meet, whether relation or stranger, whether friend or foe. All are alike to us. This was the example given to us in the lives of the great saints of modern times, Hazur Baba Sawan Singh Ji Maharaj, Sant Kirpal Singh Ji Maharaj, and Sant Darshan Singh Ji Maharaj. They saw no difference between North Americans and Asians, Africans and Australians, Europeans and South Americans. They had love for all. They saw no differences between Muslims, Hindus, Sikhs, Buddhists, Zoroastrians, Sufis, Christians, people of the Jewish faith, or Taoists. They had love and regard for members of all faiths. They saw no differences between theists and atheists. All were members of one human family.

When we recognize our spiritual unity, we will begin to care about the welfare of others. We will see that all are fed and well-cared for. We will see that all have a shelter over their heads. We will see that everyone has medical care and a good education. We will not be able to look at ourselves in the mirror if we have caused harm to any of God's creation, our brothers and sisters in Him.

If we are leaders of a religious group, we have a deep responsibility upon our shoulders. It is up to us to call for a moratorium on religious wars, religious conflict, religious bigotry, and religious hatred. It is up to each of us to live up to the example and teachings of the founders of our religion and teach universal love, unity, non-violence, and tolerance. We have the power and the duty to see that each member of our constituency lives up to the lessons of love and non-violence as taught in our scriptures. If even one life is taken, if even one drop of blood is shed in the name of our particular religion, the responsibility for that tragedy is on our shoulders if we have done nothing to prevent it by teaching love and non-violence. Each of us must look to our own selves and peep into our own hearts. Are we teaching love for all religions? Are we teaching non-violence to all humanity and to all life? Are we teaching peaceful co-existence among members of all religions? Are we teaching unity in diversity? If we do not speak these words from our pulpits and live these noble virtues in our life, for what purpose are we leading our religions? Do we think the founders of our religions and God Himself would be pleased with us? If we have been chosen to lead a congregation in any religion, it is up to us to bring God's message to our constituents. Is not God's message one of love and unity? Would God wish to see any of His children, created by Him, to be killed in His name? Let us start from this day forward and truly teach the gospel of love, unity, and peace.

If we are followers, let us also look to the scriptures and the teachings of the great saints and prophets. If we are true followers of our religion, we will live love, peace, and unity. If we are true followers of our religion, we will live our lives in such a way that we can reunite our soul with God. If we are true followers of our religion, we will spend some time daily in prayer and meditation that will connect us with the Holy Word, the Light and Sound of God within us, and travel on it back to His lap. If we are true followers of our religion, we will sit together with all members of humanity, irrespective of religion, nationality, color, or social status, and pray together as one family in the Lord.

It was the life's work of Sant Kirpal Singh Ji Maharaj and Sant Darshan Singh Ji Maharaj to bring people of all nations and religions together. In the gatherings they held at their ashrams or at public discourses in India and abroad, one could see people of all faiths united in the common purpose of meditation to realize their self and to realize God. They did not come to form any new religion. They had regard and respect for all religions. As they said, "There are so many religions already in the world. There is no need to form another religion. But there is a need to help people realize the purpose for which their religion came into being, and that is to realize their essential unity as a part of one Lord." They helped people fulfill the purpose for which their religion was established. They renewed the teachings of all previous saints and prophets by reminding humanity of the gifts already given to them through the ages. They reawakened humanity to the simple technique of inversion through prayer and meditation in order to regain their divinity.

Let us follow the advice given to us by Sant Darshan Singh Ji Maharaj in this verse:

> God has thousands of Names,
> Call Him by any Name and He will respond.
>
> He is so close to you,
> Call him, He will surely respond.

Let us sit together at this Conference, and call to Him in any name we wish. Let us call to Him by the thousands of names by which He is known. And let us all experience together the Love, Light, and Ecstasy that He is eager to bestow on each of us, who are all His children. Let His love flood our very beings and let us leave here embracing each other with God's boundless love flowing through each of us.

Birth Centenary of Sant Kirpal Singh Ji Maharaj

February 6, 1994

One hundred years ago today, God fashioned a perfect being who embodied all His godly qualities and sent him into this world to help us attain the same divine glory. Sant Kirpal Singh Ji Maharaj entered this world on February 6, 1894, as a reflecting mirror so that God's rays of light and love could shine upon every soul in creation. He was a perfect being who embodied spirituality, godliness, selflessness, universal love, and peace. When we look back over the pages of his life, we find that he called himself a man like us, but he was more than a man. What was he? He was spirituality on earth. He was all noble qualities moving on earth. He was selflessness on earth. He was love on earth. He was peace on earth. And he was human unity on earth.

We are very lucky to be here celebrating the centenary of the Beloved Master Sant Kirpal Singh Ji Maharaj. Many of us were fortunate to have met Sant Kirpal Singh Ji Maharaj during his lifetime.

For others, we learned of Sant Kirpal Singh Ji Maharaj through the Gracious Master Sant Darshan Singh Ji Maharaj. He had boundless love for Sant Kirpal Singh Ji Maharaj, and he worked tirelessly to carry his message and his memory to all parts of the world. Each of us wish that Sant Darshan Singh Ji Maharaj could have been with us here on this day. He often spoke of Sant Kirpal Singh Ji's centenary, and before he left the body, Sant Darshan Singh Ji made many plans for us for this centenary celebration. He often spoke of the centenary as one of the greatest events of this century. How happy he would have been to be here with us physically on this day! But he has not left-- he is with us all today in spirit. Sant Darshan Singh Ji has left for us these sublime words about Sant Kirpal Singh Ji in this poem:

> All glory to God that His Cupbearer is pouring forth the wine of self-knowledge.
>
> He bestows the Light of divine love;
> let us bow down to him for he is the arbiter of our destiny.
>
> You cause our hearts to blossom,
> And you embrace each and every one as your own.
>
> Your inspiring words illumine our lives,
> And your message lends divine fragrance to the universe.
>
> May the bond of brotherhood knit us all together,

> And may the entire universe be at peace
> under your protective wings.
>
> We pray that we may ever drink your cup of love
> And live to celebrate your centenary.
>
> May this tavern be forever blessed by your presence;
> We pray to the Masters for your everlasting life.

Sant Kirpal Singh Ji came to this earth with a godly mission and he was the personification of all that was divine. Yet he lived among us as a human being to show us how we too could exemplify the highest virtues while withstanding the storms and tempests of earthly life. The lessons he had for humanity were threefold: first, he lived the highest qualities in his own life; second, he found a way to encapsulize what he attained in a way that could be understood and practiced by modern humanity; and third, he established a forum which provided human beings opportunities to put the highest truths into practice in their own lives.

If we look at each aspect of his life, we will find the model, the teaching, and the practice by which each of us could do what he had done. As he often said, "What one man has done, another can also do, with proper guidance and practice." When he told us, "I am a man like you," he was providing us with positive hope that we too could attain self-knowledge and God-realization as he had attained in his life.

On this centenary, let us look back over the pages of his life to see what lessons he holds for each of our lives. Let us look at how he modeled, taught, and helped us to practice spirituality, ethical living, selfless service, love, human unity, and peace, so that we might have an illuminating lamp to guide our path into the next millennium.

Spirituality

From early childhood, he started on his search for the highest truths. He would settle for nothing less than self-knowledge and God-realization. His quest was not easy. He read through every book and scripture he could find, looking for the way back to God. He visited many a place of worship and many a holy one to find answers to his questions about the mystery of life and death. He made up his mind that he did not want to waste his life in worldly pursuits or in studying under teachers who did not lead him to the highest goal-- God-knowledge. He prayed to God to lead him to a teacher who could reunite his soul with God. When he matriculated from high school, he took a decision: God first and the world next.

God hears the sincere cries of those who yearn for him. Sant Kirpal Singh Ji was blessed in 1917 with an inner vision of a spiritual teacher, whom he took at the time to be Guru Nanak. It was not until 1924, when he happened to be visiting the Beas area, that he met Hazur Baba Sawan Singh Ji Maharaj and discovered that it was he who was appearing to him within for seven years. He received initiation into the inner Light and Sound from Hazur and found in him the Master who could take him back to God.

This example from his life shows us the one-pointed desire and yearning to find the way back to the Lord. We see how God blesses the seeker by leading him or her to someone who can put us in contact with the God Power within us. Having found a way back to God that gave sure and definite results, a firsthand inner experience of the Light and Sound of God, Sant Kirpal Singh Ji Maharaj devoted his life to the meditation practices, attaining communion with God.

When he was entrusted with the task of Naam initiation by Hazur Baba Sawan Singh Ji Maharaj, Sant Kirpal Singh Ji presented the spiritual teachings in a way that could easily be understood by people of modern times.

Sant Kirpal Singh Ji Maharaj devoted his life to making the spiritual teachings accessible to thousands of people throughout the world. Through three world tours and about twenty books in English, he made this science available to people from all walks of life in every country and in every world religion. He made it available to every man, woman, and child, irrespective of the nationality, religion, culture, or social stratum from which one came. He taught how we could make spirituality a part of our modern lives. We did not have to leave our hearths and homes to go into the jungles and caves to meditate; we could practice meditation within the confines and comforts of our own homes.

Besides giving out the theoretical side of the spiritual teachings, he also provided a forum by which people could practice meditation for themselves. He founded Ruhani Satsang or Spiritual Gathering in which seekers could come together and learn the science of meditation. They could meet him at Sawan Ashram to learn meditation, or they could go to one of the hundreds of centers he set up throughout the world and learn the meditation practice. He kept in communication with disciples throughout the world through his tours, his books, his circular letters and messages, his correspondence, and through a monthly magazine, Sat Sandesh, which carried a monthly talk or message from him about spirituality. Through personal contact with him or through letters, he helped disciples perfect their meditations so they could complete their spiritual journey back to God. He did not offer any blind belief. He gave each one who came to him a practical, firsthand experience of the inner Light and Sound, leading to an experience of rising above body-consciousness. He gave each one the method by which they could journey into the higher regions, such as the astral, causal, and supracausal planes, ultimately culminating in the soul reuniting with God in the spiritual region of Sach Khand. As he often said, "Feelings, emotions, and inferences are all subject to error; seeing is above all."

Thus, Sant Kirpal Singh Ji underwent the spiritual search in his own life; having found the fulfillment of that search he gave out the spiritual teachings in a way that was easily understandable, and then he provided a forum by which people could practice spirituality in their own lives.

Ethical Living

We see in the life of Sant Kirpal Singh Ji a model of the ethical virtues. He studied the lives of hundreds of great people and saints throughout history. He came to the conclusion that each one of them embodied noble virtues within their lives. He knew that if one were to succeed in one's spiritual quest for God, meditation was not enough. One also had to develop godly qualities in one's life. As he often said, "Truth is high, but higher still is true living." In his own day-to-day life, he practiced the virtues of nonviolence, truthfulness, chastity, humility, and selfless service.

Even before he met his spiritual Master he exemplified these characteristics. From childhood we see him refusing the meat offered to him by his parents telling them, "I do not want to make a graveyard of my body." We see him refusing to carry on the animosities his parents harbored for their enemies. As a child he told them, "Your friends are my friends, but your enemies do not have to be my enemies."

When it came time for him to present the spiritual teachings of Hazur Baba Sawan Singh Ji Maharaj to the world, Sant Kirpal Singh Ji gave it great thought. How could he help humanity live up to the ethical virtues worthy of their human existence? He came up with a system of keeping an introspection diary. He saw that great people through the ages had some way of keeping track of their behavior. He devised a diary by which people could daily evaluate how they measured up to the ethical virtues. He listed columns for non-violence, truthfulness, chastity, humility, and selfless service, and each day one would count the number of times one failed in these virtues. By noting the failures one could resolve to do better the next day. Ultimately, one could weed out these failures and end up with zero in that column. He taught the relationship between developing the virtues and having spiritual progress. The negative traits were hindrances that kept our mind from the calmness, equipoise and purity needed for accurate concentration. He showed us how by overcoming these traits we could make our mind a still pool upon which God's light could be reflected.

By providing the diary, he gave disciples a practical method of perfecting their own lives. He taught them how to use the diary, and he would have the disciples send them to him periodically for review. When disciples visited him in India, he would ask to see their diaries. He would then offer them practical suggestions on how to improve, answer their questions, and give them guidance. Along with keeping track of the virtues, the diary also contained columns for time spent in meditation, and by reviewing the time put in by disciples he would guide them and inspire them to increase their time.

Sant Kirpal Singh Ji Maharaj often said, "It is difficult to become a true human being, but once we do so, it is not so difficult to find God." Thus, he exemplified the ethical virtues in his own life, taught the importance of the virtues, and provided a practical method by which disciples could develop these virtues in their own lives.

Selfless Service

Sant Kirpal Singh Ji Maharaj's life was a model of selfless service. Even before he met his Master, he was practicing this holy virtue in his own life. When he visited his uncle in the hospital he found an old man lying ill next to him with no relatives to tend to him. Sant Kirpal Singh Ji personally would buy medicines, food, and fruit for the elderly man and would tend to him. When the lad's uncle asked him why he was taking care of a stranger, the young Kirpal replied, "He has as much right on me and my services as you do. I have come here to love all."

Sant Kirpal Singh Ji served selflessly during the 1919 worldwide epidemic of influenza, a deadly disease by which millions of people throughout the world died. When few would dare touch the bodies of those stricken with the deadly disease, Sant Kirpal Singh Ji sacrificed his own safety and tended to the sick. The disease was so feared that even relatives of the dead would not touch the bodies to bury them. But Sant Kirpal Singh assisted in burying the bodies of those who died.

After he met his Master, Hazur Baba Sawan Singh Ji, Sant Kirpal Singh Ji devoted his body, mind, heart, and soul to his service. Physically he would help with tasks such as the construction of Dera Baba Jaimal Singh at Beas. He would continue to visit the sick in hospitals and in their homes, relieving them of their suffering. Intellectually, he would help his Master with the literary work. Spiritually, he devoted himself to long hours of meditation each day. And Hazur assigned him the task of holding satsang or spiritual discourses in different cities as well as giving initiation on his behalf.

When Sant Kirpal Singh Ji had to carry forward the teachings of Hazur after 1948, he taught the importance of selfless service. He would tell us that the position of selfless service is no less than doing meditation. "Service before self," was one of his mottos. And time and again we heard him say, "As long as you are in the human body, give, give, and give."

Besides teaching the importance of service, he provided a forum by which disciples could practice selflessness in their own lives. Through the establishment of Ruhani Satsang, Sawan Ashram, and Manav Kendra he provided a chance for people to participate in selfless service opportunities. By establishing a free langar or free kitchen, people could work together to prepare meals that would feed thousands of people. He established a free allopathic, homeopathic, and ayurvedic medical dispensary not only providing free medical care and medicines to those who needed it, but allowing those with medical skills to use their services to help humanity. He established a school at Manav Kendra by which people could use their intellectual talents and skills to teach the young not only academic subjects but how to become a well-rounded human being, physically, mentally, and spiritually. In Satsang centers throughout the world, people had opportunities to give of their talents for the betterment of humanity on the physical, mental, and spiritual level. Selfless service even formed part of the introspection diary, whereby one would mark any opportunities for service that they turned down, so that the next time they had an opportunity to help someone, they would avail themselves of it.

Thus, we see in Sant Kirpal Singh Ji's life a model of selflessness, his clearcut teachings about selfless service, and a forum by which people could participate in numerous selfless service opportunities.

Love

If anyone asks, "What was Kirpal Singh like?" the outstanding quality that stands out was his love. He was love embodied. His love extended from his family to all creation. He exemplified universal love moving on earth. Whoever met him came within the radiation of his love. We could see in his own life, how he loved saints and sinners alike. Even those who tried to abuse him or even take his life were met with his love. And by his love, he transformed even sinners and murderers. People who worked for him at his office spoke of his boundless love. He treated all alike, whether superiors or subordinates. At a time when supervisors would not open their doors for the lowest workers in the organization, his doors were always open. He would take up the case of those who were on the verge of being fired. He would take the worst workers under his wings, and through love and example, he would transform them into excellent workers. When he retired from his government service, people wept at this loss. One Muslim gentleman, who was considered by others as a peon, came crying to Sant Kirpal Singh Ji. When the man was asked why he was shedding tears at his departure when he hardly knew him, the man replied, "You consider me as a man--not as a dog."

During his spiritual ministry, he spoke of the necessity of love. He would often quote, "Love thy enemies," and "Love thy neighbor as thyself." In his talks, in his writings, and in his public discourses, he stressed the need for love for God and love for all creation. In fact, love was the way back to God. "God is love, the soul, being the same essence as God, is love, and the way back to God is also through love," was one of his oft-repeated quotes. He lived up to the commandments of Hazur Baba Sawan Singh Ji who advised him once in a letter, "There are also some who indulge in tall talk and calumny; they are ever ready to slander. But our duty is to love all. If they do not give up their wicked ways, why should we leave our noble ways."

Sant Kirpal Singh Ji did not only preach love, he lived love. By his own example, by his own love, he provided the means to inspire his disciples to practice love in their own lives. He would say, "Love cannot be taught; it can only be caught, like an infection." Through his love, his disciples caught love and made it a part of their lives. He had such deep and tender concern for all those who came to him, as well as for all humanity. He was known as the Lord of Compassion. One could see the look of compassion on his face and flowing from his eyes when one told one's tale of woe to him. He not only listened to one's sorrow and suffering, he took that suffering himself upon his own body to relieve those who came to him of their burden. How many times did we go to him with our problems, and they were relieved! And how many times did we see him suffering vicariously on his own body for our sins and shortcomings! The anecdotes of his life are rich with accounts of the way he provided solace and removed from those who came to him the burdens of sickness, mental anguish, financial trouble, or troubles in worldly relationships. Seeing the love he poured out to all humanity would inspire us and ennoble us in some small way to radiate love within our own spheres. It was by his love that we all learned how to love.

Peace

Many have called Sant Kirpal Singh Ji the prince of peace. If any person exemplified spirituality, ethical virtues, selfless service, and love one would feel that person to already have lived a rich and fulfilling life. But Sant Kirpal Singh Ji's virtues did not end there. He was also the embodiment of peace on earth. In his life, he lived non-violence. Whereas another might fight his attackers, Sant Kirpal Singh Ji when faced with opposition and the threat of murder, opened his arms to those who were armed, and thus disarmed them. At a time when India underwent partition, Sant Kirpal Singh Ji opened his doors to people of all religions.

During his ministry, he worked tirelessly for world peace. On his world tours, he met with religious, civic, and social leaders, trying to get across the message of peace. As he told them, "You have the care of your consituencies under you. It is your responsibility to provide for them and to help work towards peace." He told world leaders that it was their job to stop the tides of war and to bring about peace with other nations. As president of four World Religions Conferences, he tried to impress upon religious leaders their duty to bring about world peace. He felt it was the responsibility of the religious leaders to teach tolerance and love for people of all religions.

Sant Kirpal Singh Ji provided the forum by which disciples could learn how to lead a life of peace. By everyday life at the ashram, or in the satsang centers, or by living in the modern world, he showed disciples how to deal with situations in such a way that they maintained peace and brought about peace. He gave practical advice and examples of how one could remain peaceful despite the storms and stresses of life. People would ask him questions about situations in their life, and he would guide them as to the proper way to act. He himself, when dealing with others, exemplified the highest model of peace, and those who witnessed his actions learned from them.

Thus, through example, his teachings, and the practical opportunities he provided, people could see how to incorporate the virtue of peace in their lives.

Human Unity

His life's work culminated in a major step forward for humanity. Sant Kirpal Singh Ji organized and convened the first Unity of Man Conference twenty years ago in 1974. This grand step forward aimed at uniting human beings not through religion, but through their commonality as human beings. He wanted all people to achieve unity, whether they were theists or atheists. His work laid the groundwork for many human unity conferences and organizations that came later. He is recognized today as the "Father of Human Unity." This was not mere preaching. He lived the belief in human unity in his own life. He saw no difference between one person and the next. All were human beings whether they came from one religion or another, one nation or another, or were one color or another. He treated all people with the same love, respect, and concern.

Throughout his ministry he emphasized the necessity of love and tolerance for all. His life spanned a time when racial discrimination was practiced, when there was a cold war between nations with different political ideologies, when there was discrimination between people of different social classes. His teaching of unity was a bold step in a time when leaders who spoke out for unity were often martyred. Yet he came with a mission-- the mission of love and unity.

By creating Ruhani Satsang, he revolutionized spirituality. Previously, people could only worship God with others born into the same religion as they were. Hindus could only worship with Hindus. Muslims could only worship with Muslims. Christians could only worship with Christians. Those of the Jewish faith could only worship with others of the Jewish religion. By creating Ruhani Satsang, he set up a platform upon which people of all religions could sit together in love and unity and worship the One Creator. If any of you would have visited Sawan Ashram or attended one of his public discourses on his world tours, you would have witnessed a great phenomenon. Side by side, sitting in love and harmony, were people of all religions sitting in meditation and worship of the Lord. In his assembly, all differences were dissolved and people sat together at the level of human beings, side by side in love. This was a great marvel and a miracle at a time in which two leaders of different religions would not even talk to each other, let alone sit together. Besides uniting the followers, he brought together heads of all religions in his assembly to discuss their common unity. His programs and conferences were a giant step forward for humanity. If today we see more interreligious programs, it was due to the work of Sant Kirpal Singh Ji. If today we see heads of religions uniting for the common purpose of peace and unity, it was due to the unprecedented work of Sant Kirpal Singh Ji towards these ends.

He encouraged his disciples to practice human unity in their own spheres. Thus, within their own circles, tens of thousands of people radiated love and unity to those around them. On the job, in their community, in their families, his disciples lived unity and tolerance, thus carrying his message to the far corners of the globe.

As we gather here today on his centenary, we have much for which we are grateful to Sant Kirpal Singh Ji Maharaj. If today we have a world in which there is more interreligious communication, it was due to Sant Kirpal Singh Ji. If today we have a world in which countries who followed communism and those which followed democracy are communicating, it was due to the efforts of Sant Kirpal Singh

Ji. If today we see followers of all religions sitting together peacefully in meditation and prayer to one common Father, it was due to Sant Kirpal Singh Ji. If today we see people caring about the welfare of others, for the protection of the environment, and for the peace of the world, it was due to Sant Kirpal Singh Ji. If today we see millions of people throughout the world turning to spirituality and a practical method of meditation leading to self-knowledge and God-realization, it was due to Sant Kirpal Singh Ji Maharaj.

Let us all join together in thanks and reverence for this great saint who will be remembered for millenniums to come as the one who brought about spiritual awakening. In 1974 he announced that we are witnessing the dawn of the golden age, an age of spirituality, peace, and love. If we are witnessing the rising sun of that age, it is because of the godly sunshine he himself brought to our planet. Let us celebrate his centenary by evaluating our own lives to see whether we are living up to the example of godliness he set. Let us see if we have incorporated in our own lives spirituality, ethical virtues, selfless service, love, unity, and peace. If we have not, let us start from today and make each of these qualities part of our personal mission statements of our lives. If we have, let us pursue these goals with even more enthusiasm and devotion. He has given us the roadmap by which each of us can attain God-realization and can bring about peace and love on earth. Let us fulfill the mission for which he came to this planet--to see that each of us as soul returns to the Lord and reunites as one family of God.

As Sant Darshan Singh Ji Maharaj said of him in a verse:

> Throughout His life He knew no rest;
> At home and abroad He was ever at work,
> Enkindling God's Love in human breasts.
>> How can the glory of Sawan fade?
>> How can the Mission of Kirpal fail?
>
> Let us pledge to dedicate our lives to Him,
> And for the work for which He came,
> We bow unto Him--the Lord of the Tavern;
>> May His Message spread far and wide!
>> May the dignity of man ever rise high!
>
> Let us be true to His paeans of love,
> Let us be true to the memory of Kirpal,
> Let us walk abreast in His footsteps.
>> Let us be good and engage in goodly deeds,
>> Let all mankind be knit together in peace.

And:

> You have made manifest in humanity,
>> the saving life-line of the
>> holy Light and sacred Sound;
> You have led the long-parted, lovelorn soul
>> back to her bridal-bed in
>> heaven above;
> Your celestial Light has enriched the earth
>> a thousand-fold, and raised the glory
>> of ancient India.

O! Grant us but a drop from your tankard
    divine,
    and allow us to kiss the dust of Your
    feet!

Let us all join hands in Your Holy Cause--to
    transform the prevailing gloom into
    a rosy dawn!
Let us awaken the thirst for spiritual
    experience,
    the crowning glory of human birth!
Let us share alike the joys and sorrows of
    the world,
    shedding freely the light of
    peace and amity!
Let us like radii converge at one center,
    meet in God--the live center of all!

    Sant Kirpal Singh Ji Maharaj represented what is possible for each of us to become. Let us live our lives so as to achieve spiritual upliftment, ethical qualities, selfless service, universal love, peace, and human unity. Let us follow his example in our own lives so that we can each attain self-knowledge and God-realization. By doing so, we will each be contributing to peace on our planet. If we are leaders, let us set the example of a noble life so that our followers will have a living model to follow.

    It is my heartfelt prayer to God that Sant Kirpal Singh Ji Maharaj's centenary celebration and the remembrance of his life and teachings hold high for us the model by which we live our lives in the next millennium so that we can truly usher in the golden age of love, spiritual unity and peace.

Books and Literature

By Sant Kirpal Singh
The Crown of Life: A Study in Yoga
Morning Talks
Naam or Word
Godman: Finding a Spiritual Master
A Great Saint—Baba Jaimal Singh: His Life and Teachings
The Jap Ji: The Message of Guru Nanak
The Night Is a Jungle and Other Discourses of Kirpal Singh
Spiritual Elixir
The Teachings of Kirpal Singh
Spirituality: What It Is
Heart-to-Heart Talks: Volumes I and II
Prayer: Its Nature and Technique
The Wheel of Life: The Law of Action and Reaction
Man! Know Thyself
The Mystery of Death
A Brief Life Sketch of Hazur Baba Sawan Singh Ji Maharaj

By Sant Darshan Singh
Streams of Nectar: The Lives, Teachings, and
 Poetry of Saints and Mystics
Love At Every Step: My Concept of Poetry
The Wonders of Inner Space
Spiritual Awakening
The Secret of Secrets: Spiritual Talks
A Tear and a Star
The Cry of the Soul: Mystic Poetry
Soulergy: The Source of All Energy
The Meaning of Christ
Ambassadors of Peace
Jaadah-e-Noor (Path of Light) (Urdu)
Mataa-e-Noor (Treasure House of Light) (Urdu)

Talash-e-Noor (Quest for Light) (Urdu)
Manzil-e-Noor (Abode of Light) (Urdu)

By and About Sant Rajinder Singh
Ecology of the Soul
Education for a Peaceful World
Spirituality in Modern Times (Hindi)
Illumine Every Heart
Spreading Divine Love

By Other Authors
Brief Biography of Sant Darshan Singh Ji Maharaj
Brief Biography of Sant Rajinder Singh Ji Maharaj
The Beloved Master
The Saint and His Master
Kirpal Singh: The Story of a Saint
    (compiled and adapted for children)
Vegetarian Creations
Portrait of Perfection: A Pictorial Biography
    of Sant Kirpal Singh
Ocean of Grace Divine
Seeing Is Above All
Spirituality in Action: 15th International
    Human Unity Conference

Ordering Books
Books listed on these pages may be ordered through booksellers or directly from SK Publications, Science of Spirituality Distribution Center, 4 S. 175 Naperville Road, Naperville, IL 60563. Tel: (708) 955-1200 or FAX (708) 955-1205; or through Sawan Kirpal Publications, 2 Canal Road, Vijay Nagar, Delhi 110009 India.

Sat Sandesh: The Message of the Masters
This monthly magazine is filled with practical and inspiring articles on all aspects of the mystic experience. For subscription information, write: Sat Sandesh, Subscription Dept., 19384 Smoots Rd.,

Bowling Green, VA 22427. Sat Sandesh is published in English, French, German, Spanish, Hindi, Punjabi, Marathi, and Sindhi.

SK Publications Services
For Audiotapes, Videotapes, and Photographs: Order from Science of Spirituality Distribution Center, 4 S. 175 Naperville Road, Naperville, IL 60563, U.S.A.

For Books, Literature, and Information in Different Languages:
Arabic, Bengali, Gujrati, Hindi, Marathi, Persian, Punjabi, Sanskrit, Sindhi, Tamil, Telegu, and Urdu: Write, Kirpal Ashram, 2 Canal Road, Vijay Nagar, Delhi 110009 India.

Amharic, Chinese, Croatian, Czech, Douala, Dutch, English, Ewe, French, German, Greek, Guarani, Hausa, Hebrew, Hungarian, Icelandic, Igbo, Indonesian, Italian, Japanese, Korean, Latvian, Nembe-Izo, Norwegian, Polish, Portuguese, Quechua, Roumanian, Russian, Slovak, Slovene, Spanish, Swahili, Swedish, Tagalog, Twi, Ukranian, and Yoruba: Write, Science of Spirituality Distribution Center, 4 S. 175 Naperville Road, Naperville, IL 60563, U.S.A.

About Science of Spirituality

Science of Spirituality—Sawan Kirpal Ruhani Mission is a nonprofit organization dedicated to bringing to seekers after truth the teachings of Sant Rajinder Singh Ji Maharaj, Sant Darshan Singh Ji Maharaj, Sant Kirpal Singh Ji Maharaj, Hazur Baba Sawan Singh Ji Maharaj, and spiritual Masters who preceded them. Seekers are taught the science of meditation by which they experience the inner Light and Sound, rise above body-consciousness, transcend the higher spiritual regions, and ultimately attain self-knowledge and God-realization. Science of Spirituality, whose international headquarters is located at Kirpal Ashram, Delhi, India has 900 centers in over forty countries. Seekers and students can visit Sant Rajinder Singh Ji Maharaj at Kirpal Ashram, 2 Canal Road, Vijay Nagar, Delhi 110009 India, or at the Science of Spirituality Center, 4 S. 175 Naperville Rd., Naperville, IL 60563, U.S.A. for meditation instructions, retreats, initiation, and to attend discourses, or they can meet him on his frequent world tours.

Hazur Baba Sawan Singh Ji (1858-1948): He made Surat Shabd Yoga, which had been accessible to the few, available to humanity at large. He prophesied a great spiritual awakening.

Sant Kirpal Singh Ji (1894-1974): Through three world tours and numerous books, he taught spirituality as a practical science. He was the founder-president of the World Fellowship of Religions and presided over four World Religions Conferences. He convened the first Unity of Man Conference in 1974 and laid the foundation for human unity.

Sant Darshan Singh Ji (1921-1989): He established five hundred fifty spiritual centers in over forty countries and published literature in over fifty languages. He was a renowned mystic poet and received four Urdu Academy Awards for his poetry. He presided over the 6th World Fellowship of Religions Conference and inaugurated the 15th International Human Unity Conference. He taught "positive mysticism," whereby one pursued spiritual goals while making positive contributions to the world.

Sant Rajinder Singh Ji (b. 1946): He annually convenes the Global Conference on Mysticism and the International Conference on Human Integration. He was a major presenter at the 1993 Parliament of the World's Religions in Chicago and addressed the Assembly of Religious and Spiritual Leaders. He is the president of the 7th World Fellowship of Religions Conference. He holds meditation seminars and travels throughout the world teaching people how to attain inner and outer peace through meditation.